Sassy

An Enchanting Collection Of Poems And Quotes

Rotaynda King

authorHOUSE®

AuthorHouse™
1663 Liberty Drive
Bloomington, IN 47403
www.authorhouse.com
Phone: 1-800-839-8640

First published by AuthorHouse 6/21/2011

ISBN: 978-1-4567-2835-9 (sc)
ISBN: 978-1-4567-2836-6 (e)

Printed in the United States of America

Any people depicted in stock imagery provided by Thinkstock are models,
and such images are being used for illustrative purposes only.
Certain stock imagery © Thinkstock.

This book is printed on acid-free paper.

Acknowledgments

Writing this book was not an individual project. I'd first like to thank my husband for your love and support from the very beginning.

I'd also like to thank my parents, siblings, family members, and friends for all of your encouraging words during this process.

A special thanks to all the exceptional women who have inspired me and supported this publication.

CONTENTS

Acknowledgments   v

PART ONE
Poems and Quotes   1

PART TWO (Special Edition)
Poems For Mentors & Family   71

PART ONE

REGAL

You laugh greatly at my misfortune and glee with grandeur at my proportions as you believe yours are more dignified.

Nonetheless, my expressions are those of a winner-because you are surly undeserving of my speech.

Dismayed by my stillness-sour you have become. Visibly from afar you now candidly know-my portions have no authorization to define me, but yours certainly are explicit.

BANKRUPT

My love for you was immeasurable, yet you never gave my spirit
wings.
Now, gutted I ruin as you freely stroll. My bucket lays empty on
these heartless floors.

ROOM RESERVED

As we grow we discover the energy others hold in our lives, and the vacancy they leave once they are no longer present.
Those promising moments of should have, could have, was going to, yet again evoke for voice. The void is too great to be left unfilled, with organic space unoccupied, we transform.

UNKNOWN CELBERITY

Who are you child with these frightful coiled locks?

Who are you child with ruin down shoes clapping from soles?

Child I'm talking to you.

Who are you child with these ragged garments?

Who are you child wearing these hefty bifocals?

Child just who do you think you are racing with all your might - as though you are of some importance?

Child, Child.

And the child spoke with absent tremble and a petite thunder in her voice.

"I am all you are not – Yet, everything you grudge to be!"

A WOMAN OF THE VILLIAGE

I inspire worth
I inspire trust
I inspire passion
I inspire beauty
I inspire confidence
It takes a village of women to raise a village of girls.

I advertise kindness
I advertise self-esteem
I advertise discipline
I advertise gratitude
I advertise humility
It takes a village of women to raise a village of girls.

I encourage commitment
I encourage leadership
I encourage friendship
I encourage loyalty
I encourage compassion
It takes a village of women to raise a village of girls.

I kindle change
I kindle joy
I kindle creativity
I kindle bravery
I kindle love
It takes a village of women to raise a village of girls.

CODE BLUE

She never knew what power she had until she was laying unconscious. She was powerless to the world as well as to herself-without discipline floating reminiscent of counterfeit. Her destiny was left undiscovered by the years of rebellion.

Her self-discipline if matured would have commanded power-surging an inheritance. Lacking control she wilted as if incapable of discovering her power and defenseless in pursing her destiny. As a lost lake her attraction too is void.

Her discipline could have sheltered her in a sea obscurity, except she never understood her power-now her destiny rest awaiting her arrival. Will she ever unearth her authentic power?

CREAM OF THE CROP

My standard is exceptional
My knowledge is elite
My values are supreme
My strength is immeasurable
My style is exclusive
My heart is unpolluted
My beauty is attracted to itself
My light is untouchable royalty
My faith ripens by the second
My worries are those of fowls
My wit is yet to be determine
My peace mirrors calming waters
My wealth is a portrait of generosity
My happiness is without lid
I Am A First Class Woman

BABY DOLL

Your virtue is not summed by how swiftly you divulge your essence-but by asserting it's confidentially. Given yourself without distinguish restricts absolute-which leads to further questionable provision.

Devotion for oneself can ripen by discovering who you are initially-instead of prying layers of another. Campaign for a partner with integrity, principles, and holiness—quality must be sought after.

Be watchful of those with complexities of inferiority. For their poor standard if lead in by curiosity will paralyze the psyche.

RECEIVE THE BLESSING

As I arose this morning I thought to myself how full my glass is.
For this day, I realized I am Enough, and not for the typical reasons of health, wealth, great job, or status.
For when I stood in the mirror on this day, my reflection validated me, and said "You Are Enough Just As You Are" and I received my gift of value.

INDEPENDENT BEAUTY

My brown skin is beautiful. I live in discipline.
My brown skin is charming. I don't stew in unfairness.
My brown skin is graceful. I walk in love.
My brown skin is intriguing. I play the game to win.
My brown is elegant. I thrive in uncertainty.
My brown skin is remarkable. I am a lifelong learner.
My brown skin is dazzling. I thread to own myself.
My brown skin is alluring. I enjoy sharing my knowledge with others.
My brown skin is exciting. I rotate inventory frequently.
My brown skin is mesmerizing. I network like no other.
My brown skin is power. I understand my worth.
My beauty as a black woman is just that-BEAUTY

GLAMOROUS

Welcome to your new life – go ahead and be bold.
This is your time to take ownership – take pleasure in your spotlight.
Be all you can be to yourself – it's still your time to run free with no holds.
Live loud like thunder leaving only imprints for generations to marvel.

GENESIS

Chained to the fences-I stay torched by means of a slow death.
Unlocked to flea toward new beginnings I grip tightly.
Captured by the stronghold of what if, but released again by the
smell of independence.
Victory I believe – now all I have to do is rise.

FULL GROWN

My hips are established
My mind is matured
My heart is seasoned
My plans are stable
My laughter is infectious
My goals are unwavering
My pace is prime-time
My confidence is lasting
My love is durable
My life is balanced

GOLD

Talented Sister
only your walls can stop you.
Talented sister
fly without the permission of others.
Talented sister
free yourself from regret.
Talented sister
your dreams are only the distance you place.
Talented sister
rise up and take center stage – be heard.
Talented sister
know for each door locked – you have the keys to unlock hundreds
of other doors.

Forgiveness waters your garden-without irrigation there will be no yield.

AWAKEN

Pick your feet up and get moving—life will wait for no one.

Which includes you in all your beautiful ideas—your destiny is achievable.

Don't wait for others to recognize your greatness—just take off and let them catch up to you.

The world will make room for the gifts which lie within—now is the time to make your dreams a reality.

TENDER LOVE

The core of who you are
only can be compromised by who you allow in.
Your seed is aimed to grow beautiful,
but even a small bruise can devalue the fruit.

ORGANIC WOMAN

Exquisite yet Timeless
Bold yet Humble
Powerful yet Encouraging
Beautiful yet Minimal
Energetic yet Clam
Ordinary you're not! Extraordinary you are!

Influencing yet Peaceful
Gifted yet Intelligent
Strong yet Balanced
Willful yet Purposeful
Youthful yet Professional
Ordinary you're not! Extraordinary you are!

Fierce yet Nurturing
Radiant yet Fostering
Confident yet Delicate
Luxurious yet Natural
Charismatic yet Delightful
Ordinary you're not! Extraordinary you are!

Purposeful yet Creative
Approachable yet Selective
Attractive yet Disciplined
Prominent yet Patient
Sociable yet Spiritual
Ordinary you're not! Extraordinary you are!

Sophisticated yet Vibrant
Driven yet Genuine
Constant yet Relaxed
Prestigious yet Secure
Motivated yet Selective
Ordinary you're not! Extraordinary You Are!

SURVIVOR

I still stand after the injuries.
I still stand after the neglect.
I still stand after the abuse.
I still stand after the grief.
My life is not determined by your altitude.
Therefore,
I stand in prominence.
I stand in triumph.
I stand in optimism.
I stand in authority.
I STAND IN AWE OF THE BEAUTIFUL WOMAN REFLECTING BACK AT
ME IN THE MIRROR-I STAND.

To begin lack of aim is to end without discernment.

HARMONY

Along the way girls are taught to hold on to their originality, but life has a way of defining a standard.
Girls are told to be confident-but time has a way of receding that as well.
Little girls are told to trust themselves and reluctantly others as well-without slight reservation damage is inevitable.
Tell the little girl inside,
Courageously, love yourself with no conditions.
Nourish yourself in abundance.
Habitually walk in forgiveness.
You are no longer that little girl, but a Magnificent Woman.

PURE ABOUNDANCE

No one knows my ending and few have known my beginning.
My freedom resembles a river flowing with opportunities.
Exclusively I will navigate the direction,
and my persistence will challenge the currants.
With every whisk I will wash ashore a new discovery.

UNVEILING

This moment is mine to seize.
The role I play demands awards.
I am entitled to as many takes as life will grant me.
My light from within will guide me towards perfection.
The stance I make today will evoke actions of tomorrow.
This film will be priceless.
Camera, Action, Lights.

CONFINDENCE

I trust you Lord.
I trust you.
I trust you.
I trust you.
I am committed to waiting this storm out with you Lord.
I trust you will shield me as you have done so many times before.
As the tides thump against me - I grant you complete control.
For I believe in you and know victory awaits me.

DETOUR MAN

I know what I like and I know what I dislike.
I know what I like and I know what I dislike.
I know what I like and I know what I dislike.
And at this moment it's you – please leave.

HONEST DECIET

Going through life without purpose emulates an untamed yard
without a beginning or end.
Knowing where to begin in taming the yard can be mystifying - but
once the necessity has been exposed the process is now initiated.

UNOFFICIAL GARMENTS

The greatest mistake we can make is to live in between two worlds, because we ultimately neglect the most beloved one – with no progression toward either one.
Accept who you are and where you are presently, and stop catering to a woman who has no occupancy inside your residence.

MAZE OF A MASTERPIECE

The journey of life has multiple directions.
Life allows us the freedom to choose which route.
Time will make a decision regardless of your inability to select a trail.
The art of choice is being willing to choose a pathway.

Distinguish your day by believing within yourself.

BEYOND MEASURE

My shoes wobble off in serious contemplation.
My socks nonetheless come off willingly.
My belt unbuckles wavering.
My trousers glide off effortless.
My shirt unpeels staring at the anonymous.
My undergarments dash off with anticipation.
Now standing idyllic I leap.

WORLD PEACE

I run to the left
I run to the right
I run for freedom.

I run to the left
I run to the right
I run for freedom.
I run for peace.

I run to the left
I run to the right
I run for freedom.
I run for peace.
I run for equality.

I run to the left
I run to the right
I run for freedom.
I run for peace.
I run for equality.
I run for courage.

I run to the left
I run to the right
I run for freedom.
I run for peace.
I run for equality.
I run for courage.
I run for compassion.

I run to the left. I run to the right.
I run. I run. I run.

UNBREAKABLE

You wanted to break me with your shallowness and emptiness but,
guess what-
I Persevere.
You wanted to break me with your degrading dialect but, guess
what-
I Rise.
You wanted to break me with your complexes of inferiorities but,
guess what-
I Conquer.
You wanted to break me with your rage and anger but, guess what-
I Survive.
You wanted to break me with your resentments and guilt but,
guess what-
I Maintain.
You wanted to break me with your lack of admiration but, guess
what-
I Sustain.
You wanted to break me with your shrewdness but, guess what-
I Thrive.

Investigating excuses dispatches all doubts.

Strength is not aborting your goal in sight of fear, but staying the course and profiting from it.

A dialogue with insecurity kills promise.

PRIVIATE PARTY

Today,
I'm going to honor my temple by taking a loving look at myself in the mirror.

Today,
I'm going to embrace all my quirkiness which sets me apart from others.

Today,
I'm going to compliment myself for all the beautiful qualities I possess.

Today,
I'm going to celebrate the cellulite on my thighs and marvel at the texture of my hair.

Today,
I'm going to appreciate my eye color and nurture all my facial features.

Today,
I'm going to rejoice in my beauty and admire my luxurious brown skin.

Today,
I'm going to forgive myself for what I didn't know and applaud myself for what I now understand.

Today,
I'm going to compliment myself often, admire my own beauty, and relish in my own tranquility.

A MOTHERS LOVE

My mother showed me
Love promotes.
My mother showed me
Love cultivates.
My mother showed me
Love fosters.
My mother showed me
Love respects.
My mother showed me
Love admires.
My mother showed me
Love honors.
My mother showed me
Love values.
I now share my mother with all the little girls who never learned
these valuable lessons. It's never too late to learn.

PREVIEW

If you don't believe your worth the best then you will get second, third, or whatever is left.
Giving up who you are at the expense to hold on to someone who is already gone mentally-silences the both of you!

STERILE

A filtration system goes through various steps before delivering the finished product. Unclean water becomes sanitized, fresh, and consumable after undergoing the filtration process. As we emerge ourselves into a relationship with Christ we to must go thru a filtration process.

Many times believers attempt to go into relationship with Christ were they last left off. This is an impossible task due to all the various dimensions we have experienced in this world. There is a freshness that must take place in order for growth.

The old worn out garment of unforgiveness, hatred, jealousy, and envy simply want due. Allow your relationship with Christ to process without obstruction until there is a consumable product. There is true assurance in knowing God is still working in our lives throughout the process.

SECRETS

Your love carried me when I had none of my own.
I now understand the pain I brought upon myself was unnecessary,
but the compassion you bestowed upon me was of pure grace.
You guided me back to love, compassion, and joy.
Thank you Father for your unchanging love. I'm valuable because
of you and safe when aligned with you.

EVALUATION

In this fast pace world of technology money can purchase several things including souls.

The essence of time is so fragile that it's amazing how many of us waste it doing task of unimportance.

No one could ever pay you enough money for your time because it's irreplaceable.

No job can pay you enough to become old and gray lacking memories of family.

If wisdom could be purchased in a bottle I'm sure the road of truth would have come much sooner.

You know what's even sadder is some people are still busy getting nowhere that they never figure this out.

Start today by deciding what you want out of this life and stop allowing others to decide for you.

Warranties of failure consist of pleasing others.

LIMITED PARKING

With each vehicle there comes a new untold story.
Life is a lot like a parking spot-so while parked here on earth.
You might as well enjoy your time.

MILLION DOLLARS

Once you discover your purpose- stop battling it. For every one step you take in boldness. God will take multiple ones on your behalf. Can you just take a moment to imagine how enormous His steps must be for your baby steps.

The good news is you don't have to convince Him for this promotion. He already knows your limitation and still stamps your journey access granted. God can be as big in your life as you allow Him to be.

WINNER

Indulge yourself by nurturing the woman within. Reflect on what was as well as what is. Allow yourself time to experience the changes which have occurred throughout the years. Be reassuring and sensitive to your feelings this is an emotional time.

Catering toward self will become a new exciting adventure all on its own if allowed. Begin to embrace your surroundings by pampering yourself as if you were expecting royalty to stop by. Create an atmosphere of an oasis because you are worth it. By letting go of the unused we begin to explore more about giving. But for now make a decision to begin embracing yourself with love, kindness, and respect.

ACCEPTANCE

As believers it is fundamental we know who we are in Christ. We are bombarded daily with worldly images. We lend ourselves out to others frequently, and allow them to define how our day will be played out.

The beauty of being created by God design, is simple knowing He made no two people identical. The willingness of accepting who you are, allows you to step into your designed greatness. This task is no easy one and can only be obtained by renewing your relationship with Christ daily. While pursing Him were guaranteed flowing knowledge about how we fit into His divine plan.

Take a few moments and read Ephesians 2: 8-10.

GO FOR IT

The further you push against the fears of life - the more life you will experience. Incomplete projects will only detour, delay, and eventually drown you.

This publication would have never reached your hands – had I remained disobeindent.

CASCADE

Humanity showers kindness
Humanity showers love
Humanity showers empathy
Humanity showers joy
Humanity showers patience
Humanity showers likeness
Humanity showers action
Humanity showers unity

Not bestowing confidence is the same as cheering for the opposing team.

24 HOURS

The further I push myself the more God enlarges my territory.
There have been several setbacks and obstacles along my journey
in life, but nothing worth having shows up effortless.
With every challenge I have developed more than the previous
challenge. Life will continue to exist and the path it takes will liken
on the victories I gain from each challenge.

LIFE YOUR LIFE

The life you are yearning to live is up to you.
No one can create your destiny for you.
So, if you are waiting for that special promotion on your job to embark courage to act.
Stop waiting go out right now and act.
Remember it is not up to others to discover your uniqueness it is up to you to show them.
Life will continue to pass by.
Either get in the game or sit happily on the sidelines.
The choice is yours.

DEPROGRAMING

Float in your own river of life. No matter how rough the course may toss you. Just remember the river is yours to own. What started out as a simple do I look cute in this? Has turned many people into replicas of media, print, friends, and the Jones syndrome!

The craze to ware whatever is the hottest has re-programmed our existence as well as the quality of our true authentication. God never intended for us to compare ourselves to others as a measure of our self worth.

We have all bought into this illusion of where you are-is not where you should be. Today's moguls make several daily decisions for you through media, print, and celebrities.

By pursuing happiness in items you sabotage the true beauty of life-the things that are free. Something tycoons, media, print, and celebrities just can't sell.

VIVACIOUS WOMEN

Your style is bodacious.

Your honesty is fearless.

Your smile is sincere.

Your humor is infectious.

Your friendship is refreshing.

Your love is embracing.

Your joy is radiant.

Your sincerity is understood.

Your heart is open.

Your words are trusted.

Your company is welcomed.

EXPRESSION

God created me and no matter what others think, there will only be one me.
Therefore, I refuse to allow others to define me or shape my destiny.
This journey is mine to own and the opportunity to repeat yesterday is null and void.

THE TONGUE

Words of Wisdom
Words of Kindness
Words of Strength
Words of Joy
Words of Love
Words of Destiny
Words of Hope
For we inspire the words of CHANGE.

The words from Integrity
The words from Heart
The words of one with Character
The words of Will
The words of Movement
For we propel the world of tomorrow with are WORDS.

GLITTER

I dare you to wear boldness.
I dare you to wear intelligence.
I dare you to wear elegance.
I dare you to wear dedication.
I dare you to wear holiness.
I dare you to wear charisma.
I dare you to wear values.
I dare you to wear humility
I dare you to wear character.
I dare you to wear generosity.
I dare you to wear confidence.
I dare you to shine.

MIRROR

She was once a dear friend now a distant acquaintance. I great her daily with a shallow hello-frozen by the disconnection from years of complacence-I yearn for her affection and thirst for her lost confidence.
Edging for closeness with every slight passing-yet crippled by goodbye with every forced hello.

CHAMPION

I believe I'm grounded
I believe I'm authentic
I believe I'm elegant
I believe I'm fearless
I believe I'm loved
Believing in me is always valuable
I believe I'm trustworthy
I believe I'm beautiful
I believe I'm committed
I believe I'm reliable
I believe I'm strong
Believing in me is always splendid
I believe I'm intelligent
I believe I'm confident
I believe I'm disciplined
I believe I'm important
I believe I'm remarkable
Believing in me is always fabulous

FLY ABOVE THE HATERS

Woman, lift your head and act as though you have somewhere to go.
Woman, speak as though your words are thoughtful or not at all.
Woman, walk tall with your head high or take a seat.
Woman, be either impressive or have no concessions at all.
What a privilege it is to be a woman.

SELF-INDULGENCE

In love with my brown skin
In love with my natural coiled hair
In love with my thick hips
In love with my brown eyes
In love with my wide nose
In love with my distinctive arms
In love with my smile
In love with myself

MAJESTY

Jesus thank you for your Peace
Thank you Jesus
Thank you Jesus
Thank you Jesus
Jesus thank you for your Tenderness
Thank you Jesus
Thank you Jesus
Thank you Jesus
Jesus thank you for your Grace
Thank you Jesus
Thank you Jesus
Thank you Jesus
Jesus thank you for your Friendship
Thank you Jesus
Thank you Jesus
Thank you Jesus
Jesus thank you for your Unconditional Love
Thank you Jesus
Thank you Jesus
Thank you Jesus

INVITED

You are somebody
You are Important
You are special
You have an opinion
You have intelligence
You have the right to speak

NO REGRETS

Starting where I am with what I have-not had or should have. Is my daily gift to myself.

ROYALTY

I have entered where kings and queens did so long before.
I too greeted with harps, ropes, and cheers from the crowd.
My eyes are amazed by the vast amount of wealth still very
relevant.
My feet are now planted where the king once stood.
I walk gracefully listening to the harps and appreciating the sturdy
parquet flooring.

While waiting for the servers I can't resist gazing at all the priceless
artwork which now encircles me.
My glass is full of champagne and laughter fills the quarters nicely.
Once on the lawn the cool breeze of France reminds me how far
away from home I am tonight.
While drinking more champagne I marvel at the water show, and
wildly imagine what once was and captivated by all that is.

CONSENT

I take pride in myself.
I love myself 1st.
I love my body.
I love being patient with myself.
I am a person capable of being loved and giving love.
I will not surrender to pain.
I will forgive often.
I will speak kindly to myself.
I will cherish my alone time.
I will seek to learn.

PROFITS

You are worth believing in.
You are worth adoring.
You are worth respecting.
You are worth affection.
You are worth investing in.

PINK ESTEEM

Self respect is not optional. Allowing others to determine your altitude equates to no aptitude. Being passionate does not have to encapsulate being crazy.

POWER & REWARD

No.
Not now.
Not interested.
No thanks.
I pass.
Not a good time.
Thanks, but no thanks.

MARVEL

The sound of music
Beloved
The sound of music
Treasured
The sound of music
Honored
The sound of music
Healing
The sound of music
Gratifying
The sound of music
Uplifting
The sound of music
Captivating
The sound of music
Alluring
The sound of music
Harmony

GLOW BABY GLOW

Glow for the adaptation of infancy to adulthood.
Glow for the delicate years which brought fourth your masterpiece.
Glow for the wisdom of knowledge only time could have dispensed.
Glow Baby Glow
Glow for the unknown people who width the doors of opportunity.
Glow for the bulbs which grew larger to create your purpose.
Glow for the discovery of success which matures daily.
Glow Baby Glow
Glow for the haven of peace which evokes new assignments.
Glow for the process of renewal which brings forth a cleansing.
Glow for those who moved on willing and unwilling.
Glow Baby Glow
Glow for the blooming of love.
Glow for the scares life left behind along your journey.
Glow for the fullness and abundance life offers you today.
Glow Baby Glow

PART TWO

THE VERDICT OF SOUND JUDGMENT

I can find an average or shall I say a low performing brother
anywhere.
Their fractional and the supply of these brothers are high - but the
demand is low.
Instead I focused on the purpose driven brother with an objective
and vision.
The complexity of his thinking is intricate nonetheless insightful
and sexy.
I willingly provide this brother with my affection for his assets are
well established.
He too appreciates the value of a good woman and after due
diligence closes the deal.
The measurement of our union appraises high and we both cash
in.
(Inspired By My Husband)

GRACEFUL SOLO

If I had an Idol it would be you-for my gratitude is immeasurable.
If I had an Idol it would be you-thank you for every second,
minute, hour, and day you sacrificed for our family.
If I had an Idol it would be you-thank you for your gentleness, love,
and kindness you showered me with throughout the years.
If I had an Idol it would be you-thank you for believing in me and
being my personal cheerleader.
If I had an Idol it would be you-for your noble consideration for
others taught me the true meaning of Love.
If I had an Idol it would be you - for it has been my esteem
pleasure to be blessed by your affection.

Inspired by my mother (Rita)

APOLOGY ACCEPTED

I now understand you could never give to me something you never had. People go a lifetime making excuses for their mistakes when a sincere apology may be sufficient. The pain another inflicts on someone else-could never be understood by the recipient, but the gift of forgiveness is understood by both.
I now understand you could never give to me-something you never had. By accepting your apology it embodies me with the choice to forgive. We certainly don't get to choose our parents but if I did-I still would have chosen you.
Inspired by my dad (Kelly)

GRACE

You are, an elegant woman.
You are, an elegant friend.
You are, an elegant teacher.
You are, an elegant listener.

Inspired by (Claudette, Dawn, and Silvia)

VIBRANT CHICK

She keeps the party rolling with her wild in loud laughter.
Yes she is a vibrant chick.
Her outrages stories-filters streams of fresh air.
Oh, yes she's a vibrant chick.
Quick to react but slow to judge.
She stands in her spotlight with a warm embrace for all.
Yes, Yes, she is a vibrant chick.

Inspired by my sisters (Rolanda & Nicole)

TALENTED BROTHER

Lost years are will not recycle. I wish I could take all the pain away from you as a small child, but the fact is-that pain provided you with wings for today.

Lost time is never coming back. Regrets in life are only a poor person excuses for their choices. Today graced you with the same 24 hours as the next person, and how you spend your time-will be your tomorrow.

Allow people to love you, but most important forgive and love yourself.

Inspired by my brother (Charles)

EXQUISTE

Grandparents are the most nurturing individuals.
Grandparents are the best cooks in the world.
Grandparents are composed.
Grandparents are full of wisdom.
Grandparents are a blast to hang out with.
Grandparents are inspiring.
Grandparents are teachers for generations to come.
Grandparents are to be treasured.

Inspired by my Grandparents (Ramona & Robert)

HOPE

Thank you for being an Uncle I could trust and lean on.
Thank you for watering the seeds of entrepreneurship in my life.
Thank you for your guidance and direction as an investor.
Thank you for being fun to hang out with and talk to about books, politics, and of course business.

Inspired by my Uncle (Curtis)
I pray God continues to bless you and your wife with all His greatness.

ECONOMICS

Thank you for being a teacher
Thank you for being a leader
Thank you for believing in your students
Thank you for your encouragement
Thank you for your guidance
Thank you for your wisdom

Inspired by (Mr. Crawford)

SERENITY

God is not done with you yet. He still has more to teach you.
God is not done with you yet. He still has more He wants to bless you with.
God is not done with you yet. He still wants to be the number one priority in your life.
God is not done with you yet. He still needs you to trust him without your assistance.
God is not done with you yet. He stands waiting to breathe fresh air into your life.
God is not done with you yet. He is willing to heal any ailment.
God is not done with you yet. He is waiting to bestow you with more wisdom.
God is not done with you yet. He is waiting to bless you like none other.

Always, remember when the liar comes to attack you-God is not done with you yet, and you can trust-what He started He will finish.

Inspired by my Stepfather (Aston)

FREE

God is your gift-allow him to use you.
God is your gift-allow him to free you.
God is your gift-allow him to lead you.
God is your gift-allow him to heal you.
God is your gift-allow him to develop you.

Inspired by (Dennis & Michael)

EXCEPTIONAL WOMAN

The Oprah Show
Has been a voice for blind
Has been a physician for the sick
Has been a therapist for families
Has been an education vehicle for the world
The Oprah Show
Has brought unparalleled inspiration
Has brought unparalleled awareness
Has brought unparalleled knowledge
Has brought unparalleled advocacy
The Oprah Show
Has saved lives
Has saved homes
Has saved girls in remote countries
Has saved marriages
The Oprah Show
Has given her audience and viewers lifetime memories
Has given her audience and viewers peaks into the lifestyle of the
rich and famous
Has given her audience and viewers education for generations to
come
Has given her audience and viewers the tools to promote action
and make lifelong changes
The Oprah Show
Audience has grown up with her for these past 25 years and will
miss seeing her dearly weekdays at 4:00pm
The Oprah Show
Audience has shared 25 years of experience together with Oprah
and watched her bloom into this rare find
The Oprah Show
Audience has lost weight with Oprah, gained weight with Oprah,
and accepted our weight with Oprah as well
The Oprah Show
Audience has revealed the most intimate details of their lives to
allow growth, awareness, and advocacy for all of us.

The Oprah Show producers, writers, and staff will all be immensely missed.

Oprah you are in a league all alone and deservingly so. Your kindness, compassion, and strength have been irresistible to us all. Thank you for being a phenomenal woman and sharing the past 25 years of your life with the world.

Here's what I know for sure, you will be a success in all your business endeavors and your legacy will have an impact on multiple generations. Your commitment toward education will continue to inspire villages, cultivate leaders, and escalate the world toward a better tomorrow.

Goodbye to the Oprah Show and Hello to OWN.

Goodbye to the Oprah Show and Hello OWN.

CHAMPION

Thank you for displaying beauty in all sizes.
Thank you for giving us the movie Just Wright, and showing
women around the world their beauty is theirs to own.
Thank you for giving us the movie Last Holiday, and challenging
viewers to live more passionate lives.
Thank you for staying true since UNITY.

REMARKABLE

To my First Lady you are:
Impressive
Appreciated
Exceptional
Rare
Honorable
Meticulous
Sophisticated
Trustworthy
Distinguished
Composed
Peaceful
And oh yes, Fashionable

Thank you for doing an astounding job. Behind every good man stands a Great Woman.

JOURNEY

To all my angels who have made an investment into my life.
I sincerely say thank you-for without your deposits of love,
inspiration, compassion, hope, and thoughtfulness on my behalf
this book would not have been possible-Thank You.

www.ingramcontent.com/pod-product-compliance
Lightning Source LLC
Chambersburg PA
CBHW030406290526
45785CB00004B/1918